Letters to My Ex

Letters to My Ex

Marvin Barnes

authorHOUSE®

AuthorHouse™
1663 Liberty Drive
Bloomington, IN 47403
www.authorhouse.com
Phone: 1-800-839-8640

First published by AuthorHouse   1/29/2010

ISBN: 978-1-4490-7702-0 (sc)

Library of Congress Control Number: 2010901091

Printed in the United States of America
Bloomington, Indiana

This book is printed on acid-free paper.

The title of this book derived from thoughts of past encounters with women that left an impression on my behavior and outlook. I believe the way we love is built upon past experiences and the consequences and desires that remain as residue after those encounters have long since past.

M

Addict

Inquisitive of whether I'm an addict
Helplessly trapped by my desires
Still capable of rationalized thought
But able to dismiss its very rationality at my whim
I attempt to prevent this strong compulsion
Yet I find surrender so suitable for comfort
My want quickly becomes a need
My need only necessitates images or thought
Then I become a victim of uncontrollable desire
A desire that takes a life of it own
One in which control isn't an option
Consummation becomes my reality
Inquisitive of whether I'm an addict
Access is freely given sometimes demanded
Satisfaction requires a repeat performance
Exceeding expectations elicits addiction
I wonder whether you are an addict
Calling me for one purpose
Saying you love me when I know you don't
Making excuses for me when no one should
Forgiving me for anything after ecstasy is complete
Satisfying all my erotic fantasies completely
Doing the things that you do

Inquisitive of whether we are addicts
Dismissing family and friends for secret pleasure
Ignoring love ones and unimportant responsibilities
Rationalizing this as love when we both no better
Pretending this pretense is any logical form of reality
Becoming available at a moments notice for pleasure
Desiring each other like children when we both know we shouldn't
Inquisitive of whether I'm an addict
Whether I can't help myself or do I want to
Whether I was born like this or this is learned behavior
Whether I am a slave to my desires or whether my desires can ever be a
      slave to me
Questions of whether I'm addicted to something innate in you
Something that requires me to need you temporarily
Perplexed at the possibility of becoming addicted to being addicted
Contemplation of these thoughts persist
Comfort refuses to stay in the shadows
Exposing futile attempts to suppress u
Desire becomes an inferno
Until my body acknowledges your presence
I am then completely satisfied until the next ember ignites
I wonder whether I am an addict?

AM

I woke up this morning and I didn't love you
No emotion no sorrow no feeling
No lingering for your smile or whispering of your voice
Devoid of the feeling of passion or regret
Finally a feeling of peace tranquility
I imagined this morning would be dark
A perfect picture of gloom
The birds wouldn't be singing
The sky no longer blue but pale gray
I envisioned no children's laughter
I envisioned all the contemporary pieces of living a futile existence
I envisioned desperately missing you
Instead I awakened to new possibilities of unfulfilled promise of me
A slimmer version of myself
I shed deceit, lies, neglect and selfishness
I felt the emphasis of a weight being removed
That would begin to allow me to soar once again with those with wings
So I could begin my journey to find peace
Yes I loved you yesterday for the last time
In that time the imagery was different
Love would not allow me to see you
Only that promise of perfection that I wished you to be
Love perpetually lied to me
It hide the real you behind that façade
Not allowing me to see what was always right before me
Loves vagrant, a jester of feelings
Not aware of your worth
Never hesitant to degrade yourself willingly
Yes, this morning I awakened and I didn't love you
I loved me

Cause and effect

My heart eclipses into periods of insanity
Institutionalized thoughts that I cannot trust
Delusional feelings that require rationalized thoughts
Love and lust become constantly interchangeable
Passion becoming the catalyst of regret
Love becoming the reason to satisfy the question
The question becoming the reason to satisfy love
I'm advised what I should feel and I notify my heart
My heart attempts to satisfy my request
But is unsuccessful because success requires substance
The absence of emotional substance leaves physical isolation
That isolation demands another request from my heart
My heart requests time to evaluate whether this is real
But love isn't reality it should remain a fantasy
Fanatical aspirations of love and its expectations of eternal happiness
Pictures of a wedding dress or a straight jacket
Insanity transforms white images into disorganized thoughts
Feelings that I can't trust foreign remembrances of pleasure and pain
Images of your silhouette and the passion that is burned into my being
Knowing those images aren't love or are they
Ultimately my heart will become confused the lines blurred
The answers to the question will not matter
Only the ecstasy of the exploration
My heart eclipses into periods of insanity and it seems I am the cause

Daydreamer

Imagine all aspects of love were returned
Imagine you finding your soul mate on your first try
Imagine love that never produced tears
Imagine love as substantial as a fairytale
Imagine love without hurt or pain
Imagine love without regret
Imagine love with both participants giving 100%
Imagine love without the prospect of infidelity
Imagine love where you were your partner's reflection of beauty
Imagine love where I'm sorry was never necessary
Imagine love where security was without question
Imagine love with you as the primary benefactor
Imagine love that fulfilled all your needs
Imagine love where you were not ashamed
Imagine love that was eternal
Imagine love that supplemented your happiness
Imagine love that was the catalyst of your joy
Imagine love that comforted you when needed it most
Imagined love that necessitated I do
Imagine love that grew simultaneously
Imagine love that allowed you to understand its premise
Imagine love when your new baby smiles back at you
Imagine love on mother's day
Imagine love when it's not expected
Imagine love just because
Now stop imagining and experience it

Dreams

Predictable references of your status
Floating thru my cerebral spaces
Denying room for lesser thoughts
Prohibiting reflective consideration
Demanding to be acknowledged
Requiring intense emotional acknowledgment
That you are still at this moment necessary
That I can't will you away or ignore u
Refusing me to deny what I feel when u r n my spaces
When you are what's keeping the rhythm of my heart
I close my eyes and u appear automatically
As if I have summoned you without provocation
Flying above my thoughts toying with my desire 4 u
I drift off to sleep and I dream of u
Dreams so real that they become an alternate universe
I awake happy then I realize the mockery of dreaming
The fallacy of transitional belief in images and feelings
That were never tangible nevertheless emotionally real
My reality is filled with the practicality of love
The realism of you and the possibilities of imperfections
In my dreams there's only black and white
Reality contains too many colors too much room for error
It becomes apparent to me I love you in my dreams

Eclipse

For one to examine thoroughly its takes patience
For one to understand one must possess compassion
For one to be hurt thoroughly one must have loved first
For there is no game of chance where the stakes are direr
To love unselfishly means to leave one vulnerable
To become the victim of chance, the fool of predators
But without unselfish love one really doesn't commit
One has really never loved only participated
Love requires more than being available
The premise of love defies definition, defies reason
It's the substance of fairy tales and cupids arrows
It's the success of jewelers and hallmark
We symbolize it by giving the gift of flowers
A flower whose own minuet lifespan symbolizes love
What if love was a myth and lust was reality
Would we all be safer?
Would we begin to understand our partners within reason?
I do believe love is as beautiful as a rainbow
But it has to rain before the rainbow appears
What foolish person searches for a rainbow without rain
True love is has rare as a solar eclipse
It happens but you better not look for it every day
And when you are blessed enough for it to happen to you
Instead of the sun shining bright and everything's beautiful
The moon covers the sun
And in the darkness you are allowed to see what the light was hiding
And if you're lucky the one U love will see in the dark too

Fairytales

As an adolescent I was read fairy tales
A depiction of love manufactured by dreamers
Fantasies of perfection and perpetual returned emotions
Of dreams never being crushed living happily ever after
I was asked to buy into this world
By television programs and romantic movies
By the anticipation of a fairy tale ending
By therapists and Oprah, by hallmark and FTD
I was asked to buy into this illusion without question
Asked to blindly trust another individual with my spirit
Trust that this individual had read the same fairy tales as I
But more importantly understood them as I
That two hearts can only be balanced by one scale
With the same calibrations and responses
Allowing both to contribute equally
To understand what we see is only a presentation
And substance requires depth, a deeper look
To understand in reality it is true
Fairytales are just stories that haven't ended
That love takes work and dogmatic persistence
That nothing about love is a fairy tale
For those that have perfected it
Have understood their partners unselfishly
Or have offered the best of themselves to another without question
Each of these instances requires hard work and commitment
Something that a fairy tale lacks
Sometimes viewing love as a fairy tale can damage the process
True love is reality at its best without shortcuts or illusions
The hard work is what makes it real, makes it tangible
Allows one to appreciate it more than a fairy tale
As a child I read a book, I'm still looking for happily ever after

Falling 4 U

Autumn leaves descending rapidly as the landscape changes
Winds that whisper as they simultaneously send a shiver through me
The chill of the air elicit icy thoughts that evaporate as I remember u
The trees stand naked b4 me and I smile as I reflect back to last night
I begin to interrogate my feelings and the logical answer is u
Fall is full of promise and possibilities and the beginnings of u

The essence of your scent becomes the envy of lilacs
As flowers begin to bloom so does the reality of my feelings
My senses are never so alive as when I am with u
The inauguration of leaves hastily cloth the trees
I think of you and what's underneath… your mind
I become conscious that fall's possibilities are now spring's realities

The heat of our exploration is blazing out of control
Unquenchable nights that we incessantly attempt to recapture
Unfortunately the heat also illuminates the frailties of this union
This light exposes what the two previous seasons concealed
That we are physically compatible and emotional trainwrecks
That beyond the vertical exploration we r horizontal strangers
It begins to rain and the heat cools….Summer's almost over

The chill from you has transgressed into bitter cold
You desire to talk and become startled by my frost bitten lips
Our feelings have become frozen because we couldn't survive the
        inclimate weather
This cold rapidly kills all promise of a brighter tomorrow
I attempt to light the fire and fail the same as you
We begin to look forward to a spring without each other
Our love couldn't survive this winter
I never could understand the Fall

Fantasy

I'm in love with a fantasy
No, not an image of perfection
That my heart and mind has conspired to facilitate
an aura of utopia
Not a masculine perception of visual admiration
Or a fool's reflection of unblemished stature and beauty
No, as with all my dreams my fantasy is deeply entrenched in reality
My image of perfection is instilled with flaws and promise
My fantasy is of you
Not an unrealistic desire for the perfection of you
But the privilege of being with you when you are at your best
My fantasy is to be the source of your smile
The shelter in your storm
My fantasy is to be your reason
For you to be my first three wishes
My solitude, my purpose
My fantasy is for your heart to realize
When I think of you
Reality ceases to exist

Flashback

I miss you
I can't seem to stop thinking about you
My mind perpetually returns to thoughts of you
You leave me with a feeling of longing
One that requires your presence
I can still smell your fragrance in my sheets
Your soft breath on my neck
I still see your smile
See the light in your eyes
Still feel you warm in my arms
The smile when you first see me
The completeness I find with you
The security you offer
The companionship I feel with you
The way the world disappears when we are together
The way I miss you even when you are here
The sense of loneliness when you leave
I miss your thoughts
The way you allow my world to make sense
Your optimism when I'm jaded
The way we communicate
I miss all the seconds wasted before I knew you
I miss the way u make me better than I could ever be without you
I miss you and I'm blessed that it's only temporary

Forever

Childhood reflections of innocence
Heart alive with promise open to possibilities
Love was fresh and unblemished
Concepts of companionship devoid of baggage
Clandestine nights on the phone
Daydreaming of you with anticipation
Meeting your family without apprehension
Saying I'm sorry and meaning it
Listening to our favorite song
Walking with you through the hallways
Our first date preceded by our first kiss
Defending your honor
Pretending to do homework together
Missing you when we were grounded
Thinking our parents don't understand
The deep belief that my life would end without you
Walking you home from school
Leaving my friends because I couldn't wait to c u
Your parents trusting me with you
The look on your face when I asked you to be with me
The look on mine when you accepted
Dressing as a couple
Getting jealous for no reason
Buying your first gift with pride
U saying that tonight your parents wont be home
Us believing it would be like this forever

Game over

Delusions of you for such a prolonged period of time
Belief in an abstract image of a reality that never existed
Faith in your decency as a human always unrealized
Trust in you that was never warranted
My previous thoughts of the pain caused by your infidelity
Were attributed to the wrong that you perpetrated against me
But my feelings for you were always purely unselfish
So much that unbelievably my greatest sorrow
Was not the wrong you did to me
But the lack of your self worth
To have to realize that someone used you and you allowed it
This violation of something that I held so sacred
To fall from a pedestal that was so low that your feet touched the ground
To have no remorse for what you allowed others to do to you
To what you have done to me, but more than that what you have done
     to yourself
By being so blind as to damage what you saw in my eyes when I looked
     at you
To make me feel a fool for ever believing in you
For having to now look at you in disgust and shame
For me having to see a potential in you that was never there
For all the wasted effort when I thought you just needed me
For me not being capable of seeing through you sooner
For you accepting my love as a weakness
For me unable to stop loving you as I say goodbye

Gravity

Questions of improprieties of past indulgences
Distrust of sincere displays of emotional involvement
Quest for reparations of past violations of the heart
And you're available, available for the redemption of previous violators of
    spirit,
of broken promises and shattered dreams
of crushed self esteem and temperance of free will,
You're still here before me to accept the ungratefulness of a hardened
    heart
For your veracity to be questioned and your love overlooked
You are here because you choose to relinquish your love
to an unattainable unavailable shell of the person that you choose to
    possess
If you had arrived sooner when my heart was new and unblemished
by the games and disrespect, by the neglect
before it was perpetually broken and then shattered into unrepairable
    pieces
I could have understood you, I could have accepted you for the beautiful
    person you are and I could have recognized your love

Or maybe if my heart were brand new you would be the one that
    shattered it
Because love is imperfect
and what you love now is the unavailability of my heart
The very thing that draws you to my heart is the same imperfection that
    makes it unavailable
Maybe what gravitates you to my heart is your need to repair something
To establish your worth and if it was perfect you would need to
    manufacture an imperfection
So you could be satisfied with your repair,
With your thought of owning me because of that repair
And your need to have me repay you for your good Samaritan efforts.
 I once had the heart of a child inquisitive and forgiving, overflowing
    with love with a desire to give it to someone worthy
But that was my mistake; I should have been selfish and that heart will
    still be flying

Images

Visions of you in another life
Accompanied by me in another world
My vision insists that your mind is as naked as your body
Anticipating my next command
 My request, my desire to quench this thirst
 That only your wetness can satisfy
 I open my eyes and you stand before me naked
 I weaken as my breath leaves my chest
 My pulse quickens and I realize at this moment
 I am grateful to be a man
But with that fragility my first impulse is to conquer you
Right then the room brightens
I look up and I notice it's the light from your smile
It softens all of me except one part
That can only be reduced by your satisfaction
As I ponder my next act you stop smiling
I see something in your eyes
So familiar to me, oh yea I remember now
Erect breasts, quickened pulse, finger pulling
, Lips, biting, grabbing, tasting, passion erupting,
bodies glistening, primal moans, shuddering torsos
, throbbing, moist, wet, warm, inviting, clinging,
scratching, hair pulling, nibbling, pleas, licking,
toes curled, volcanoes erupting …………...Surrender.

Invasion

Not prepared for your violation of my heart

For the subtle invasion of the aspiration of dreams the realization of
needs

Anticipation of the inferno of passion the proximity of your flesh
facilitates

Conflicted by the thought that your mere presence demands the
prospect that there has to be another level of satisfaction

Locked within me that has been waiting for your sigh

Your shorten breaths, your quicken heartbeat, your tear,

Your lost inhibitions, your yes, your rapid pulse your surrender

Your call out to a higher being at that moment that it begins to rain

For me to feel a pleasure so intense that a part of me dies each time I
give it and I willing surrender to death

As long as I am allowed to please you with my last breath

Kissing you I lose all sense of time and rational thought

Unaware of my surroundings, my lips have purpose

My world is balanced on the tip of your tongue and I fall once again

As I did the first time you smiled, I held your hand or was intoxicated by
your voice

I realized then my heart had abandoned me and became a willing slave
to you

Kaleidoscope of thought longing for wishes that this love transcends
time

Defies rational thought, exhausts all passion and desire and becomes
your foundation

Inferno

Fragmented pictures, unfocused memories of you and me

Distinct memories of passion colorful vivid pictures of pleasure

The torrid essence of satisfaction springs from the page with the scent of you

Passion and pleasure that remains unyielding except to its two participants

Gladiators in this ring of desire and lust amid the quest for temporary satisfaction

Uncontrollable desires and scripted fantasies played repeatedly but never the same

In an arena I used to own, until you, until I found the equality that offers perfection

Your touch electrifies every nerve in my body and exposes me as an innocent child

Willing to earn your approval even if I have to stay after class and repeat the test

As I admire your body I disavow every image except this one before me

And I long to examine every inch of you as slow as you will allow

I want to hear you moan, scream, beg, say my name, is that selfish of me?

If so then I want to moan, scream, beg, say your name

I kiss your neck softly and you quiver and you pull me close

I nibble your ear and you sigh and I smile

I slowly kiss you neck on my way to your shoulder you gently touch my face

I kiss your shoulders from let to right pausing slightly so you can feel me

Rigid, hard, standing tall proud before you longing for you to make me vanish in you

Plunge repeatedly over and over drown in your pool of never-ending
   satisfaction
Feel your body react beneath me in front of me as I pull your bended
   hips closer
Pull your hair bite your neck as you make me forget the meaning of life
As the sound of your moans tell me my only purpose right now is to
   satisfy you
You're like a furnace now and your heat commands me to slow down
   take my time
I'm attempting to maintain control slow my pace but you wont allow me
You thrust, buck, while your body demand I match you move for move
 I bite my lip must contain my composure…no, I got to let this go…cant
   hold it
I change positions to buy more time, wrong move, now I see your body
Glistening before me, perfect, a visual and a sexual work of art
I refuse to let you down. …Damn I refuse to let me down
My body's on automatic now as I copy your rhythm get lost in your eyes
You say no and shake your head I say no and bite my lip once again
You say you first, I say no you first, our bodies are now moving at a
   frantic pace of undeniable pleasure,
I didn't know that pleasure could be reached at this level
   this is no longer sex, or making love, this is something new
A pleasure that allows me to feel colors and visualize heat
Our bodies are no longer two but one moving in unison
Primal, unashamed, violent, reaching for what we both no is coming
Cuming, cuming, cuming… Damn

Just another pretty face

Looks that could crumble an empire
Aspiring Cleopatra and Juliet to envy
I admire your visual perfection and it leaves me breathless
Your silhouette demands the attention that I am but so happy to give
As I look at you I manufacture dreams and unavailable promises
I desire wishes and fairytales and a promise of tomorrow that includes u
I listen and I hear only that which pleases me and refuse to acknowledge
    frailties
My belief is that these frailties don't matter and that u r the greater good
I begin to hope without foundation that u r as beautiful as your looks
In the meantime my eyes seem to be the dominant force of my being
This visual exploration is so effortless and everything else pails in
    comparison
My decision is to get to know u see if u r her
Whether there is any substance behind those beautiful features
Maybe you r like the others only a portrait a flat surface
Attempting to make it through life on gifts given 2 u by your parents
With your appearance as the only collateral for any achievement that
    may b given 2 u
Those, which I have looked for substance and found eminent
    disappointment
She that lacked personality, compassion or a thought of her own
Whose beauty left her restless for the next compliment or validation of
    her beauty
One whose value was determined by others assessments of her attributes
Her whose spirit that has been so destroyed by her unaccountability
I admire u once again and this time I c the person behind the beauty
This time I am saddened by the wasted potential of what could have
    been
Disappointed that inner beauty was never cultivated or allowed 2 grow
Forever realizing the truth that if I close my eyes u become irrelevant
Finally realizing that we both are victims of just another pretty face

Circus

Disillusioned because my heart was actually functional
Disenchanted into believing you could elevate yourself to human
Saddened by my belief that you were capable of decency
A product of your surroundings that you have come to relish so
In reality your worth is only relevant vertically
Insignificant within reality a useless toy
The appearance of potential quickly faded
Replaced with visual conformation of your worth
Idyllic aspirations shattered, shadows confirmed
Questions of faulty reasoning because u were persistently transparent
Hope allows one to ignore transparency hope demands blind belief
Thinking that what you required was someone to believe n u
To see beyond your damage acknowledge what's underneath
Astonished that underneath was an illusion and reality was the damage
That illusion was all that was left of the remnant you would never
     become
Wondering what you bartered for your morals honesty and self-respect
Mistrusting belief that I could have ever noticed any redeeming qualities
     n u
Flashbacks of a circus clown and the ringmaster
Of all those who entered into the arena and u gave a ride
The hyenas still laughing at me
Me believing you and ignoring the elephant
The strongman and the sword swallower
And my favorite of all the fat lady singing

Listen

You say you love me
Three small words
With endless implications
That require belief
Belief that u require
Words meant for effect
To solicit emotion
To repay reparations
Words meant for understanding
To provide comfort
To establish security
To justify feelings
Words meant for surrender
To establish boundaries
Words to suggest forever
You say you love me
Three big words
With a hidden agenda
That r meant to deceive
Words that damage
Words that destroy
Words that manipulate
Words that r forever dishonest
Words that kill dreams
Words that prevent
Words that solicit laughter
Words that alter
Words that deny promise
U say u love me
And I hear you

Lois

I imagine the outcome before I see u
The anticipation of u almost unbearable
Fantasies and ecstasy whose only reference is from our last encounter
Silhouettes and actions that primarily should be impossible to repeat
Even so we continue to repeat this euphoric dance effortlessly
Unscripted and unrehearsed but each performance it's own masterpiece
Each performance leaving me needing an encore
Requiring you like an addiction that I can't shake
Reality of suppressed, denied emotions spring to life
Love and lust finally at this moment work perfectly in unison
This space that we occupy becomes a separate universe
U look at me and ask what's wrong and I think 2 myself that u possess
    my rib
But I look in your eyes and smile and reply nothings wrong
As I lay with u I think forever with u would be 2 short
I smile again as I think how much I love u but I remain silent
I imagine us in a perfect world and I momentarily find myself fulfilled
I hold you in my arms again and this time imagine u safe with me
I become inquisitive about your feelings and whether u r truly aware of
    mine
I hear the minutes inside my head ticking telling me it's almost time 4 u
    to go
I instantly feel the void in my life begin to resurface as I once again
    accept reality
As u prepare to leave I wish for more time but understand its
    unavailability
You open the door and our universe disappears and the world resurfaces

Love

You tell me you love me and anticipate my reply
As if I I'm even remotely aware of the concept
Is it because I smile at you and spend time with you
Is it because I've met your family spent the night
Stroked your hair kissed you softly on the lips
You are wrong I am no scholar of love and its nuances
Just because I read poetry and buy romantic gifts
Because I have sensitivity and respect for you
Because I hold your hand when we walk in the rain
Because I call you baby and look in your eyes
Is it because I am aroused by your touch
Because I don't cheat or lie to you
Maybe its because I introduce you as my woman
Is it because the sex is incredible
Is it because I truly care for you
You wish me to recite these words back to you
And if I fail does it mean I don't love you
If I do, does it really mean that I love you
Are we supposed to find out we are in love on the same day

Maybe I'm a late bloomer and I'll find out tomorrow
I think I'm a late bloomer but I finish strong
Two people never love the same
Maybe my like is has strong as your love, I'm intense you know
What do I really know about love
I am still trying to do this right
I'm still trying to keep you from being mad at me
Still trying to put down the toilet seat, philosophically
Still trying to speak to you without talking
Is love an adverb maybe a pronoun
You just cant spring I love you on me and expect instant harmony
We need to at least practice the melody first
I'm the strong silent type a man of few words
Alright baby at least explain love to me first
Does your definition of love stop if I don't say it back
Or will your love wait for me
Will it leave me if I'm not ready
And if needed will your love just be my friend
Really what do you mean when you say I love you?

Mirage

U remained a invariable mirage
Yielding a glance but never understanding
Always before me but never tangible
Constantly available to quench my thirst
If I had only known I was parched
It took miles to realize you
With each step new revelations
With each revelation a new step
Your mere presence made the heat bearable
Illuminated dark misconceptions
Resuscitated trust and true emotions
Because I believe u are real
Even when I closed my eyes U remained constant
When my vision was hazy I knew where to find u
Inspired me to continue to aspire
Picture my oasis, my refuge, my retreat
Now picture you

Mirror

Quest for sanity of purpose
Reflections of memories of you
Weightless aspirations of security
Hopeless dreams of my reflection
Never appearing as the exact reproduced image
Fragile pieces of fractured glass looking back at you
Two-way substance leads to a single interpretation of the truth
The sun shines light on self-imposed misconceptions
Edges that cut those that love you
Streaks of love that have long since disappeared
Focused on your feelings on the ceiling
As I attempt to escape from those throwing stones
Those that wish to break me render me useless
Never understanding that this issue should be handled with care
I've already suffered through my seven years of bad luck
Now I'm ready to face myself again
Endless and repetitive shattered hopes of fulfillment
U once thought these objects were closer than they appeared
As I reflect back they were always distant
Images of you and pleasant remembrances of the funhouse
Distorted fantasies conformed to our whims
Contortions of love and lust only we can untangle
A likeness of the reality of you and me

More

Why can't I remove you from my thoughts?
Separate myth from reality fact from fiction
Fantasized versions of pleasant times
Remembrances of an alternate reality
Commitment to self-inflicted misery of you
My mind refusing to accept the truth
Unwilling to conclude love can be wasted
Questions of personal frailties of perception
Providing value to someone who was morally bankrupt
Unable to trust myself for being deceived for so long
U accepted truth as a prop, love as validation that you were proficient at
   lying
Compassion as conformation of your heartless actions
Not knowing that love has to be lived up to
That once love becomes reality when it loses that dreamlike quality
When we are cynical that love can't be greater than its present state
When we fail to believe and lose interest and compassion
When we are left with the deficiency of trust and respect
Well, Love becomes you, love becomes aborted
It's never allowed to grow, to flourish, to reach its pinnacle
It leaves all whom come in contact with you to wonder what if?
Love becomes terminal and damages anyone that it is unfortunate
   enough to touch
Leaving casualties of emotional destruction in its wake
Fractured dreams and aspirations of a better tomorrow
No, I don't wish to see you
Your repeated attempts are insulting to us both
Conversations are futile without honesty
Being honest, u treated me like you were a whore
I deserved more

MUSE

Whirlwind of thoughts containing distant memories of you
Recycled emotions of remembered pleasures
Of excited touches, overwhelming anticipation
With you as the nucleus of my being
As the facilitator of emotional bliss
Tortured events that perpetually confuse my world
I unwilling to feel, to submit to the pressure, the essence of you
Yet still gravitating to your heart like the earth around the moon
Questions of the meaning of life and love
Does love exist or is it no more a figment than the Easter bunny in a
      furry suit
Is love's only purpose to civilize the masses?
Or is it life's greatest riddle with no answer
Maybe love is the answer if so what is the question
Consider uncontrollable thoughts, unexplainable actions
The inability to think or eat
The illusion of a premise that's as accessible as water
Yet as elusive as a passing thought
If one could understand love as well as Shakespeare
One then would truly be lonely
For to understand any one thing raw and at its essence
To love and commit without fear without thought
With a total disregard for the thought of others
To offer your heart as a ritual sacrifice without hesitation
To allow your mouth to mimic your heart without filtration
That is the Alpha and omega of love
My quest is to offer you Shakespeare on a platter
And then each day thereafter alleviate his existence
By exposing him as an amateur as an imposter of love
Displaying to you what I feel for you
Makes his very thoughts insignificant
Exposing you as my muse, love's greatest inspiration

Necessity

Its difficult to conclude I never knew you
Injured but not damaged by your game of hearts
Bewildered by your conclusion that it was valid
Valid to destroy ones opinion of you
Valid to trample on your self worth
Valid to not even consider the destruction u caused
Valid to dismantle a dream
You view your transgressions as an accomplishment
As an achievement that you are desired
That you are wanted that you are necessary
Never understanding that basic premise has flaws
Your necessity is not based on need but on want
Want is always temporary never constant
Want is exchanged for the next available model
Need is constant it stands before the preacher
And her mothers smiles as she whispers I do
Wants agrees to I do as it desires something else
Want by its very nature has an appetite
One that can't be satisfied no matter what you feed it
Want is a fleeting memory Need is a requirement
Want is the premise upon the introduction
Need always becomes the final act
It takes no skill to be wanted just availability
Need requires substance demands respect
Need will make you bow down on one knee
Buy a ring, call when she's not there
Want allows you to call her to her knees
Final question since u have all the answers
Do you need me to want you?
Or want me to need you?

Proposal

Photographic surreal images of beauty
Images of your smile the warmth of your lips
Hidden contentment of you in my heart
Holding me hostage no escape
Satisfaction of your pleasure
Hope in your distress
I wonder what your beauty feels like
A thorough image of perfection that u cant escape
One that allows me to live my dream
I picture your parents young and in love
That love created you it created me
For all that I know of love completely lies in your eyes
All I ever wish to know is fabricated in your acceptance
Your love is my present and future, yesterday never existed
Everything before you has been a dress rehearsal
Yesterday was only relevant because it allowed me to prepare for you
Allowed me to understand that you are life's gift to me
Explorations of the things that allow you to permeate a smile
My heart always breaks at the same time as yours
If I cant repair yours then mine is worthless
Knowing that happiness for me is impossibility if u don't feel the same
U used to invade my thoughts now u are my thoughts, my breath
Your heart is more beautiful than u r, as I look at u I wonder is that even
    possible
I'm allergic to your tears if my heart stops your smile will always give it
    life
Until then…..Marry me

Request

I apologize for my indiscretion
Believe me it was without malice
It was only a product of thoughtlessness
My apology is sincere
But what I am sorry for is
The hurt I caused you
That your belief in me has been shaken by my actions
That my trust has been questioned in your eyes
I sorry for ever having to say these words to you
I'm sorry for the tears I see in your eyes as I apologize
I'm sorry that you ever had to question my commitment to you
For even the appearance of me letting you down
I'm sorry because that I can't make this to never have happened
Sorry because this has threatened our union
I'm sorry because I let you down
I'm sorry for the position my apologizing has put you in
I'm sorry for falling short in your eyes for even a second
I hesitate to request favor in your eyes at this moment
Instead I request you give me a chance to make reparations
A chance to make myself worthy of your trust
A chance to assist in the alleviation of your hurt
To prove I am that man you once believed in
A chance to prove that this was only an absentminded mistake
A chance to restrengthen our bond
I apologize but please give me the chance to prove I'm sorry

Unexplainable

Reactionary thoughts crowding my world
Feelings that r so new they require explanation
Explanations that wont substantiate their meaning
Words that could never convey their impact
 Never rationalize the gravitational pull on my emotions
The conflict of the ever-present battle between my head and my heart
While you become a dominant presence in my thoughts in my reason
Requiring me to solve the puzzle of my discontent
Suspending happiness within the balance of probability
Questions of how did we arrive here and was I conscious
What method of insanity allowed this to become a possibility
Remembrances of past pleasures and pain and no solutions
Moments of splintered answers to useless questions
Where happily ever after was yesterday
This is just ever after and we probably will never return to happily
While what I feel continues to return to u like a revolving door
Realizing that I have a desire for u that is impossible to quench
Understanding this love this passion this us is rare
That the masses will never experience it never understand
The impossibility of feelings that are so intense that there is no logical
    explanation
Feeling that don't require an explanation they are self-explanatory
Finally understanding that the explanation is us

Sunny Weather

Anticipating this feeling to pass knowing it refuses
Refuses to allow me comfort instead it requires me to need
Need something I have had previously
Something that I once felt was my own
Someone that I anticipated needed me
Required me, someone that felt the same desire has I
Maintained the same dreams and aspirations of hope
Needed the same confirmation of our love
She, which found the same happiness in the smile of a child
I, which shuddered under her slight touch
That breathed with her same hesitant breath
I, which was in love with her silhouette
Because my passion was 3 dimensional and undisputed
She, in whose smile I found comfort and whose arms I experienced
    solitude
I, whose dreams began and ended with her presence
She, whose very presence demanded that I become a better man
I, whose dreams of me always wished to live up to her image
Always fearful of failing her, letting her down
I, unlike she could not see beyond the stars
Still I felt this love for her that persisted that I obtain that which
I had yet to see, become what those before had failed to live up to

Settle her sprit, calm her heart build her trust, tear down those walls
And only then could I not only speak the language of love
But understand her definition, become a companion in her world
That up until this point she traveled alone
Those previously were not of the caliber to produce comfort or the
warmth that was needed to completely thaw her heart and become
the primary benefactor of this treasure she was willing to offer so
unselfishly
Those that would confuse her gifts with weakness and entitlement
I, who wanted to see what see saw but my vision was blurry,
And my appearance of mixed emotions was merely a barrier to
camouflage my fear from feelings that were foreign to me
For emotions that were offered to me that I couldn't believe in
My barrier was not to protect me just the opposite the barrier was
To protect you, from me letting you down if I never reached the stars
Form hurting you for my failure and for diminishing my worth in your
eyes
It was never I, only she
Because while she had me in the stars I still had to look up because I
knew it was there she would be

Unfinished

Stolen glances, slight touch, clandestine kiss
Remembering your heat your scent
Fulfilling unquenchable fantasies reoccurring dreams
Smoldering text messages producing guilty smiles
Undressing you with my eyes before my hands reciprocate
Searching frantically to see if u r wearing something special 4 me
And if so how will I ever reward u, over and over again
Anticipating the excitement of u exposing my favorite body part
U whispering in my ear words I only allow u 2 speak
That laugh, that smile that ignites foreplay
Your silhouette that demands attention immediately
And my body feels like immediately isn't soon enough
Unfinished glasses of wine unaware of their participation
Slow music that's about to produce thunder
Lace thong, the only thing that's going to keep u safe now is kryptonite
Curves that migrate into smooth ebony flesh
Clothes become the enemy and are slowly discarded
And you become my primary interest my solitude
…Stand there for a moment just like that
Picasso had no idea of what to paint
I need to just appreciate U for a moment
No, let me come to U….wait I got th…
Thi…this…Damn…Do your thing
Every nerve in my body relaxes except the one u control
And you have control down to a science
Reposition your body restructure your emotions
Allow your eyes to close force you to bit your lip
Quiver your hips clutch the sheets cradle my head
Your body shudders than stops.…..unfinished

When I'm gone

Eternity was never reality
Even though what I feel for you will remain
We loved ahead of our time
 I remember when I first saw your face
When you first smiled at me
The moment I realized I loved you
Forever is never promised
Even though we couldn't continue yesterday
U made my todays more beautiful
The future is always a dream
Our future was never realized
 Still we lived our dreams everytime we were together
I learned to love u n the present
Making every single moment with u unforgettable
Appreciating u every second that was given to me
Learning to love you all over again with each new day
Exposing the truth that u r my happiness
As memories of our past become our only future...smile

Wings

I sense the feeling that is not allowed under the circumstances
So I surpress it I quench the vulnerability of my heart for sanity
For a reality that I don't want to exist that I never asked for
But this reality was presented to me offered to me
Thrust upon me like some declined invitation of a solution
A solution to a problem whose answer was scientific
Logical, when the issue is one of pure emotions
Emotions that must be removed from the sphere of selfish needs
To the reality of now to the investment in another's dreams another's
    needs
To watch another's life through a looking glass and wonder what
    happened to me
To become so unselfish with someone I know should be mine
To visualize her with someone else receiving her love her warmth
To hear her softly say those three words that used to be reserved for me
To watch her grow into the person I always knew she could be she would
    be
But to observe her reach that destination with someone else
Sanity becomes a blur emotions begin to deceive
What I thought I knew about love could be contained in a thimble
I listened to her instead of my desire and she spoke
Conclusions were made images were shattered
She just needed time; time would tell her what I thought I knew

Everything we went through could only lead to one conclusion
That destination was us…we…. our…. together
They say life happens while you are planning for it
While I was planning, hers began and she accepted it
I answered the phone…. I answered the phone
The voice on the other end of the receiver
A voice that sounded so familiar
Stated that the ms. I used to know was now a Mrs.
Life hesitated for a minute then a moment
Time become frozen I never heard that
That is impossible…illogical… not believable
Visions of a white dress and a happy groom
A smiling bride saying I do
Reality pending but it's going to take some time
Fast forward to the future
A future where I can accept maybe he makes her happier than me
Maybe he is what she needed; maybe she would never be this person
      without he
Understanding love needs to be unbridled released and be allowed to
      soar
To it's highest heights and realize sometimes love will elevate above you
To someone else and when it does for the one you care for
Let her fly take solace that she found wings and she's happy

Ghost

I'm right before you but you don't see me
Your reality consists of a different me
One that you manufactured with no assistance from me
Your us consisted of a me that never existed
The fallacy of us is that your truth is based on fiction
You've made me a fabrication of the desires of your heart
A sanitized image of me achieving your expectations
Assumptions of my feelings in your favor
You have assumed a happy ending before we have acquired a proper
    beginning
I'm not disappointing you
U never took the time to know the real me
Your hallucination of me is whats disappointing
I'm an actual person not a figment of reality
But that is of no consequence if u r blind
You'll continue to see a me that was never there
Continue to see availability that was never available
To see love before it has had time to blossom
Still wonder why it's not working
Open your eyes I'm right before you
Understand this is the only me I have to offer right now
Maybe if you see me and me and slow down we'll arrive together
Even if we don't we may still enjoy the journey
The repetition of those three words still won't make them authentic
Giving your heart unfortunately doesn't mean it's going to b accepted
Understand I have to accept you before I accept your heart
And with that said you must b able to see me before u ask 4 mine

Empty

I offer generous thoughts of the past
Questions without answers
Stories without endings
Hurt without provocation
…and I forgive

Never questioning what could have been
Forever knowing that this was the only possible ending
I grasp at proverbial straws in an effort to establish reason
Knowing that reason evaporated many seasons ago
And was replaced by self preservation
…and I understand

Still I fantasize of a more suitable ending
One maybe of a better you, a better me
One in which time slaps each of us in the face
with the reality of loss before we posses the ability to lose
One in which the alternate ending has us both smiling together
…. and I regret

I wake up to a beautiful day that's far less beautiful without you
And I make the best of what's left
I attempt to show her love and compassion
And now I'm good at it
…and I think it should have been you

I buy a paper and the woman next to me flirts and smiles
She's beautiful yet I feel nothing
but that you are my world
I run home to you
…. and you're not there

First date

Excited thoughtful glances concealing truth
The waiter brings desert leaves us vulnerable to ourselves
Clandestine Dialogue spoken only within our minds
Obstructed with manufactured smiles and counterfeit laughter
One participant thinks then the other retaliates
If only these thoughts were exposed
Then we would understand the ingeniousness of this situation
She thinks we would have beautiful babies
He thinks one last child support payment and I'm home free
She thinks my feelings I could really love him
He thinks I'd love to see what's under that skirt
He thinks this could be the one
She thinks he better be more of a man than the last one
She thinks I going to take it slow get to know him
He thinks I know what I want and she's mine tonight
He thinks we could spend quiet evenings at home
She thinks I love going out with my friends
He thinks if his roommate is not home maybe he'll get lucky
She thinks you are too old to have a roommate
She believes that love should be unconditional

He thinks that sex should be unconditional
She wonders does he love his mother
He thinks of course I'm a mama's boy
He thinks I just spent 70 dollars on dinner she knows what's up
She thinks he's such a gentleman
She thinks I'm going to make him wait he'll respect me more
He thinks you better not play me for a sucker or this is the last supper
She thinks I had to show him that others were interested
He thinks she has other interests that she showed him
Reintroduction of the waiter and the bill
She doesn't even consider looking at the check
He checks the fact that she hasn't considered
He would have appreciated the gesture
She appreciated just her
This evening requires compensation and he gives it
They hold hands as they leave deciphering the smiles
Never knowing the thoughts of the undercurrent
Oblivious to the impending reality of their differences
The busboy cleans the table preparing for the next illusion

Someday

Impossible to deny your presence
A visual temptation I couldn't resist
You were unaware I even existed
A disappointment I would have to correct
Grace filled movements a smile that I had to earn
I wanted to become part of your world
Introduce myself to your dreams become a permanent presence n your
    empty places
Become acquainted with you make your reality flawless
Understand with this attraction I want to make love to your thoughts
    and desires
Sex is only relevant once this is complete
If I allow you to remain this fantasy then I would be a child
A man makes his fantasies a reality
I introduce myself hoping that u could b my someday
Someday in the rain I will hold your hand
Someday when you cry I will stop your tears
Someday I will be the reason for your smile
Someday when you dream I will be your wind
Someday u will be all that matters n my world
Someday I'll b coming home 2 u
Someday I'll buy you a ring
Someday u will say I do
Someday we'll be blessed with a child
Someday our love will make others smile
When I first saw u I was hoping someday could begin today

Hello,

First of all I would like to thank you for taking precious time from your lives to examine my material. The inception of this project began with my best friend supporting and encouraging me to write down some of my thoughts. Without that initial belief and support I would have never attempted this. My best friend happens to be a woman and until this point in my life I thought it was impossible for a man and a woman to have a solid platonic friendship. I'm happy she proved me wrong her friendship is one of my most important treasures.

I love woman, no I mean I love women, and I don't apologize for that or ever offer any explanations to those that don't understand the dynamics of my relationships, I believe if you give a woman a choice with all the facts involved you would be surprised at some of the decisions she might make. Once feelings are involved whether emotional or physical only the two participants make the rules.

What I attempted to do with this book is to cover love the good times as well as the bad. Some of my writings you may find a little raw, but love sometimes is raw when you are hurt and you are attempting to get through it. Sometimes the pain lets you know that you are still in love. I think what one has to remember is love does contain pain at some point and its how you choose to deal with that pain that determines whether your love will last or not. As I stated if you could feel the love in some of my writings I hope you feel my pain as well and understand that is still love I'm just trying to find my way back.

My attempt was that you would hopefully remember a past relationship or a past love in your reading. Maybe even offer you a different perspective on the one you care for. I will share with you some of my thoughts while writing. The line I remember most from these writings is the line from empty when I talk about "love slapping you in the face with reality of loss before we possess the ability to lose." Looking back on lost love and finding that moment where you could have salvaged your relationship and made it stronger. Where someone could have showed you what you were about to let go. Where you could feel the regret of your decision before you made the mistake of prematurely giving up.

Gravity is really about a person not ready to love that is maybe still hurt by the wrong done in a previous relationship. This individual's hurt is still so present that they can't appreciate the love that they are receiving from the individual that they are currently with. In essence they don't see that they are subconsciously sabotaging a relationship with someone who really loves them.

Invasion I wrote on the phone, my girlfriend at the time put me on hold and I began writing what I was feeling about her.

Listen I wrote this concerning the damage those three little words could do if you don't pay attention. Today we hear I love you so much that we have to question the motives behind the sentiment. When there is a lack of sincerity, and still the possibility of belief on the recipient's part damage will occur.

The Poem" Love" anyone that has ever dated me would state that was a self-portrait, and unfortunately they would have been right. Those were my true feelings during the majority of my relationships in the past.

I do believe in the love that they write about in fairy tales. But for the most part like a fairy tale that is love from a spectator's point of view. That is what you think you see when you see a couple that is extremely happy and you wish you had the type of love they have. But at this point you are just a spectator you can't observe them behind close doors when they are alone and see all the work they put into their relationship to make it look so effortless to outsiders. You don't know about the tears and the instances when they wanted to give up. The only difference between their relationship and yours is that they refused to give up. They both understand that they love each other and sometimes it takes work but what they have is worth the effort. Those couples that last remember that sacrifices are involved and sometimes your partner's feelings are the most important thing in this world if they are giving you the same in return. I guess all I am trying to say is judge your relationship on its own merit not outside influences because what you think you see could very well be an illusion. Your relationship could look just like that fairytale to another spectator if you put in the work. Hopefully something to think about.

One Love
Me

About the Author

Marvin Barnes graduated from Park University with a BS in Business Management. Mr. Barnes was born in the Chicago area and now resides in Northern VA.

www.ingramcontent.com/pod-product-compliance
Lightning Source LLC
Chambersburg PA
CBHW050344290526
45785CB00006B/2630